SLEEP LIKE YOU MEAN IT

A No-Nonsense Guide to Better Rest

Elias Grant

Asher Rohi Publishing

asherrohipublishing.com

Copyright

Copyright © 2026 Elias Grant.

Published by Asher Rohi Publishing.

asherrohipublishing.com

First Edition, 2026

All rights reserved.

No part of this book may be reproduced, stored in a retrieval system, or transmitted in any form or by any means — electronic, mechanical, photocopying, recording, or otherwise — without the prior written permission of the publisher.

ISBN

Ebook: 978-1-923781-03-0

Paperback: 978-1-923781-04-7

Paperback (extended distribution): 978-1-923781-05-4

Table of Contents

How to Use This Book

This book is short by design. Each chapter targets one specific aspect of sleep — the environment, the evening routine, the morning anchor, the food and drink decisions, the anxious mind — and gives you research-backed tools you can apply today.

Read it through once to understand the whole picture. Sleep is a system, and understanding how each piece connects makes every individual change more effective. Then go back and implement one chapter at a time. Start with Chapter 3 and Chapter 5 — your sleep environment and morning anchor produce the fastest measurable results. From there, work through the rest in any order that fits your situation.

The exercises at the end of each chapter are short and specific. Do them. The difference between reading about better sleep and actually sleeping better is whether you act on what you learn.

Two weeks of consistent implementation is all it takes to feel a real difference. This book will show you exactly what to implement.

Introduction

The Problem Is Not What You Think It Is

Here is the thing nobody tells you about not being able to sleep. The trying is making it worse. Not metaphorically — mechanically. Sleep onset is a passive physiological event. It occurs when the arousal systems of the brain fall below a specific threshold. When you lie in the dark working at sleep — monitoring your own alertness, calculating the hours remaining, willing your mind to quiet — you are maintaining exactly the level of cortisol-driven activation that prevents sleep from beginning. The effort to sleep is, neurologically, the same as the effort to do anything else. And effort is wakefulness. Sleep researchers have a name for this: psychophysiological insomnia. The defining feature is not any inability to sleep in biological terms. It is a learned association between the bed and arousal — built up through nights of lying awake trying — that makes sleep onset harder the more earnestly it is pursued. The people who fall asleep easily are not trying harder than you. They are not trying at all. They have simply not learned to try. This distinction matters because it means your sleep problem is not a sleep problem. It is a wakefulness problem. Something is keeping your arousal systems activated — or has trained them to activate — at precisely the time they should be winding down. And until you identify what that something is and stop doing it, no amount of chamomile tea, magnesium gummies, or lavender pillow spray will make a durable difference.

This book identifies the specific things keeping you awake. All of them. And it tells you, in plain English, exactly what to do instead.

* * *

Sleep is not a behavior you perform. It is a process your body runs — automatically, efficiently, with a sophistication that thirty years of sleep research has only partially mapped — whenever the conditions allow it. Your body isn't the problem. Your conditions are.

The conditions that sleep requires are specific and biological. Your core temperature needs to drop by one to two degrees Fahrenheit in the hour before sleep onset. Melatonin — the hormone that signals darkness to your brain — needs to rise without interference from blue-wavelength light. A neurochemical called adenosine, which has been building in your brain since you woke up, needs to be present in sufficient concentration to overwhelm your brain's alerting circuits. And the two systems that regulate all of this — your circadian clock and your homeostatic sleep drive — need to be in alignment, which requires, above almost everything else, consistency.

Most people's lives are providing exactly the wrong conditions. Not through carelessness — through the specific collision of modern habits and biological machinery that evolved over millions of years in a world without electric light, smartphones, or the particular kind of relentless cognitive engagement that the modern economy demands from the moment of waking to the moment of collapse.

You are not failing at sleep. You are trying to sleep in conditions that were not designed for it.

*　*　*

Here is the insight that makes every chapter in this book make sense. Your sleep problem is almost entirely upstream of your bedtime. The quality of your sleep tonight was substantially determined by what happened this morning — whether you got outdoor light within thirty minutes of waking, whether you got up at the same time as yesterday, whether you had your coffee before or after the cortisol window that produces natural morning alertness. It was shaped by what you consumed this afternoon — specifically, whether any caffeine is still blocking adenosine receptors in your brain as you try to sleep. It was shaped by what happened in the ninety minutes before you got into bed — whether your nervous system had time to complete the transition from daytime arousal to night-time readiness, or whether you were on your phone until the moment you closed your eyes and expected unconsciousness to follow.

By the time you lie down, most of the important decisions have already been made. The bedroom is the last five percent of the system. This book covers the other ninety-five.

* * *

There are two things this book will not do.

It will not cure diagnosed sleep disorders — sleep apnea, narcolepsy, restless leg syndrome, or clinical insomnia meeting the full diagnostic criteria. If you have been sleeping poorly for longer than three months, are experiencing significant daytime impairment, and have applied the evidence-based approaches in these pages without improvement, see a sleep specialist. There are conditions that need clinical attention, and this book is not a substitute for that.

And it will not offer you a hundred small tips. The sleep advice ecosystem is full of tips: try a warm bath, try blackout curtains, try the 4-7-8 breathing technique. These things aren't useless. But they are surface interventions — comfort measures that do nothing to address the biological systems driving the problem. This book goes to the level of mechanism. When you understand the mechanism, the behavior change becomes intuitive rather than effortful. You won't need to remember the advice. You'll simply not want to do the thing that was making it worse.

* * *

Here is who this book is for.

You are a professional who gets into bed exhausted and lies there for forty-five minutes, unable to understand why your body is refusing to cooperate. You fall asleep easily on the sofa, but the moment you intend to sleep, something reverses. You wake at 3am to a mind that has apparently been waiting for quiet in order to begin running through every unresolved problem in your life, in no particular order, with apparent urgency. You're a parent who can't remember the last morning you woke before the alarm, refreshed. You're a shift worker whose circadian rhythm has been in open conflict with your schedule for years. You're someone who slept well, once, and can't quite identify the point at which it stopped working. Or you're someone who has simply normalized being tired. Who's accepted that running at seventy percent is just the cost of a full life. Who has stopped expecting to feel rested and started working around the deficit instead.

That normalization is the most quietly damaging thing chronic poor sleep produces. Not the dramatic impairments — the reduced reaction time, the impaired memory consolidation, the 60 percent increase in amygdala reactivity that makes you more irritable and less patient in ways you notice but cannot always explain. The subtler cost: the creeping acceptance that this is simply how you feel now, and that there is nothing to be done about it. There's everything to be done about it. And most of it can begin tonight.

*　*　*

What follows is seven chapters, each addressing one specific dimension of the sleep problem. Read it straight through first — the chapters build on each other, and understanding the whole system makes each individual change more intuitive. Then go back to the chapter that addresses your most acute problem and implement its exercise first.

The changes are specific. The science behind them is clear. The results, for most people who apply them consistently, arrive within two weeks. Your body still knows how to sleep. Let's stop getting in its way.

Chapter 1

Why You Can't Sleep — The Real Reasons

It is 11:43pm and you're doing everything right. The bedroom is dark. You have been off your phone for twenty minutes — almost. You are lying in the position that usually works. You are telling yourself to relax. You are not checking the time, except you just did, because you need to know how many hours you will get if you fall asleep in the next fifteen minutes, and now you are calculating, and the calculation is not helping, and you are telling yourself to stop calculating, which requires thinking about the calculation, which means you are still calculating.

You aren't relaxing. You're performing relaxation. And the performance is making everything worse.

Here is what is actually happening in your brain at this moment — and why understanding it is the most important thing in this book.

* * *

The Problem Most people who sleep badly believe, on some level, that the problem is psychological. That they are worriers by nature, or too stressed to switch off, or simply not built for good sleep in the way that some fortunate people are. They have tried the behavioral fixes — the routines, the supplements, the screen-time rules — and found them insufficient, which has reinforced the belief that something more fundamental is wrong.

The belief is understandable. The conclusion is wrong.

The real reasons most adults cannot sleep are not psychological in origin. They are biological — the result of specific disruptions to two systems that govern sleep with the precision of a biological clock, disruptions created by specific modern habits that those systems were never designed to accommodate. Once you understand those systems and those disruptions, the solutions are not just intuitive. They are obvious.

The Science Your sleep is governed by two biological systems operating in parallel. The first is your circadian rhythm. Driven primarily by light — specifically by the presence and absence of blue-wavelength light detected by specialized cells in your eyes — your circadian clock regulates the release of cortisol in the morning, which wakes you and sharpens your thinking, and melatonin in the evening, which signals to every cell in your body that darkness has arrived and sleep should follow. The clock is extraordinarily precise. Under natural conditions — rising with the sun, no artificial light after dark — it runs on a roughly 24-hour cycle that synchronizes almost perfectly with the natural day.

Under modern conditions — LED screens emitting bright blue light until midnight, blackout curtains preventing morning light from entering the bedroom, irregular wake times that shift the clock forward and backward from day to day — it does not.

Matthew Walker's research at UC Berkeley documents what happens to the circadian system when it is consistently misaligned: melatonin release is delayed, core body temperature fails to drop at the appropriate time, and the brain remains in a state of biological alertness long past the hour when it should be winding down toward sleep. The result feels like insomnia. This isn't insomnia. It's a clock that's been set to the wrong time. The second system is your sleep pressure system. Throughout the day, your brain accumulates a chemical called adenosine — a byproduct of neural activity that builds steadily from the moment you wake. As adenosine concentrations rise, they produce the increasing pressure to sleep that most people feel as the day progresses: the mid-afternoon slump, the heavy-eyed feeling of late evening, the pull toward the pillow by 10pm. Adenosine is the reason sleep eventually becomes irresistible. Caffeine does not give you energy. It blocks adenosine receptors — the sites in the brain where adenosine binds to produce sleep pressure. The adenosine is still accumulating; you simply cannot feel it. When the caffeine clears, the accumulated adenosine binds all at once, producing the crash that caffeine drinkers know well. And caffeine has a half-life of five to seven hours — which means that a 3pm coffee still has half its adenosine-blocking effect at 8 or 9pm, when your body should be generating the sleep pressure that pulls you toward rest.

Research from the University of Groningen found that a single 200mg caffeine dose — roughly one strong coffee — taken at 3pm reduced slow-wave sleep quality by 17 percent even when the subject had no difficulty falling asleep. The damage was invisible from the outside but measurable in the brain.

* * *

The Reframe Understanding these two systems produces a fundamental shift in how you think about your sleep problems.

You are not a bad sleeper. You have a well-functioning sleep system operating in conditions it was not designed for. The artificial light that delays your circadian clock is not a personal failing. The afternoon coffee that blunts your sleep pressure is a choice you made without knowing its consequences. The irregular wake times that shift your clock from day to day are the result of trying to survive a schedule that your biology did not design. None of this is your fault. And all of it is fixable.

The interventions in this book aren't sleeping tips in the conventional sense. They are precision adjustments to a biological system — each one targeting a specific disruption with a specific correction.

* * *

The Concept: THE THREE SLEEP DISRUPTORS Most adults who sleep badly are being disrupted by one or more of three primary mechanisms.

The first is circadian misalignment. The clock has been shifted — typically delayed — by late-night light exposure, inconsistent wake times, or both. No amount of willpower, supplements, or relaxation techniques can override a circadian system that is timed to the wrong hour.

The second is blunted sleep pressure. Adenosine accumulation has been suppressed, typically by caffeine, by daytime napping, or by insufficient waking hours between sleep periods. When you get into bed at 11pm after your last coffee at 4pm, your sleep pressure is lower than it should be. Sleep requires a certain threshold of adenosine pressure to arrive and sustain itself.

The third is cortisol intrusion. Cortisol — the primary stress hormone, which should peak in the morning and decline through the day — is being artificially elevated in the evening by stress, by phone use, by bright light, and by the anxiety about sleep that poor sleep itself creates. Cortisol at night is the biological opposite of sleep.

Most sleep problems are a combination of all three. And each one responds to specific, practical interventions.

* * *

The Method: YOUR SLEEP AUDIT Before changing anything, spend three days tracking your current sleep. For three consecutive days, note: what time you had your last caffeinated drink; what time you last looked at a screen; what time you got into bed; approximately how long it took you to fall asleep; whether you woke in the night and for how long; what time you woke; and how rested you felt on a scale of one to ten.

Three days. No changes yet. Just data. At the end, you will almost certainly see one or more of the three disruptors in operation. Those patterns are the targets.

* * *

The Exercise Tonight, before you go to bed, set a recurring alarm for the same wake time every day for the next fourteen days. The same time. Every day — including weekends.

This single step — consistent wake time — is the most powerful intervention in sleep science for re-establishing a stable circadian rhythm. It is also the one most people resist most strongly, because it feels punitive rather than restorative.

It is not punitive. It is foundational. Every other change in this book is more effective when your wake time is consistent. Set the alarm. Keep it.

* * *

Chapter Summary

Your sleep is governed by two biological systems: your circadian rhythm (driven by light) and your sleep pressure system (driven by adenosine accumulation). Both can be disrupted by specific modern habits — and both can be restored.

Most adult sleep problems fall into three categories: circadian misalignment, blunted sleep pressure from caffeine or napping, and cortisol intrusion from stress or evening phone use.

Caffeine blocks adenosine receptors, not tiredness itself. Its five-to-seven- hour half-life means afternoon caffeine is still active at bedtime, reducing deep sleep quality even when you fall asleep normally.

Consistent wake time is the single most powerful sleep intervention available. Set one tonight and maintain it for fourteen days.

Chapter 2

What Actually Happens When You Sleep

You have probably heard that adults need eight hours of sleep. You have also heard that this is a generalisation, that some people do fine on six, that quality matters more than quantity, and that what your smartwatch says about your sleep stages is probably accurate.

Most of this is incomplete in ways that matter enormously for understanding why poor sleep has the effects it has — and why the solution is more than just spending more hours in bed.

Here is what is actually happening on the other side of consciousness.

* * *

The Problem Almost nobody understands their own sleep. They know roughly how long they sleep and whether they feel rested afterward. They do not know what different sleep stages accomplish, or why the timing of those stages within the night matters as much as the total duration.

This ignorance is costly. It produces choices — the late-night deadline, the early alarm, the weekend lie-in — that make no sense once you understand what sleep is actually doing. Understanding your sleep architecture is not a luxury. It is practical knowledge that changes what you are willing to protect.

* * *

The Science Sleep is not a uniform state. It cycles through distinct stages — each performing specific restorative functions — in a pattern repeating approximately four to six times per night.

Light sleep is the brief transitional period between wakefulness and deeper sleep — primarily a gateway, not particularly restorative in itself.

Slow-wave sleep, also called deep sleep or NREM sleep, is the most physically restorative phase. During slow-wave sleep, growth hormone is released in its largest daily pulse, repairing muscle and tissue. Cerebrospinal fluid flushes through the brain, clearing the metabolic waste products that accumulate during waking hours — including amyloid-beta, a protein associated with Alzheimer's disease. The immune system performs critical maintenance and energy stores are replenished. Slow-wave sleep is heavily concentrated in the first half of the night.

REM sleep — rapid eye movement sleep — is the phase during which most dreaming occurs, and it is as neurologically active as waking. The brain consolidates memories by transferring them from short-term hippocampal storage to long-term cortical storage. REM sleep is also when the brain processes emotional experiences — replaying them in a neurochemical environment stripped of the stress hormone norepinephrine, which is why sleep consistently reduces the emotional charge of difficult memories. Neuroscientist Matthew Walker calls REM sleep "overnight therapy." Research by Els van der Helm and colleagues at UC Berkeley confirmed that one night of REM sleep significantly reduces the emotional intensity of distressing memories — a process that does not occur in sleep-deprived individuals. REM sleep is heavily concentrated in the second half of the night.

The practical implication of this staging is profound and almost universally unknown. If you sleep from midnight to 6am, you get six hours — but you lose approximately 60 to 75 percent of your REM sleep, which clusters in the final two hours of an eight-hour cycle. Cutting sleep short is not like cutting a movie short, where you miss the end. It is like cutting a movie in a way that systematically removes every other scene. The experience is not simply shorter. It is fundamentally different — and biologically costlier — than what you think you are getting.

Research by Hans van Dongen at Washington State University found that people who slept six hours a night for two weeks performed as poorly as those who had been kept awake for 48 hours straight — and critically, they did not know it. Their subjective assessment of their own alertness did not match their objective performance. They believed they were adapting. They were not.

* * *

The Reframe This is the most dangerous aspect of chronic sleep restriction: it impairs the very self-assessment mechanisms that would tell you it is impairing you. The reframe is not "I should sleep more." It is: every hour below your biological requirement is not just making you tired. It is measurably reducing your cognitive performance, your emotional regulation, your immune function, your metabolic health, and your long-term brain health. Sleep is not a luxury that ambitious people sacrifice. It is a biological necessity that, when skipped, extracts a cost you cannot see but are absolutely paying.

* * *

The Concept: YOUR SLEEP ARCHITECTURE Understanding your sleep architecture means understanding that the timing of sleep stages within the night is as important as the total duration. Slow-wave sleep — front-loaded into the first half of the night — is when your body physically repairs itself. The brain's waste clearance system runs its most thorough cycle. Growth hormone peaks.

REM sleep — back-loaded into the second half of the night — is when memory consolidation occurs, emotional processing happens, and creative connections between disparate pieces of information are formed. Cutting your night short with an early alarm primarily cuts REM. The implications for memory, creativity, and emotional regulation are significant.

Alcohol interferes with REM sleep specifically — suppressing it for the first half of the night and producing a REM rebound in the second half that fragments sleep and creates vivid, disturbing dreams. The relaxing effect of alcohol at bedtime is real but brief; the sleep architecture damage persists all night. Knowing this changes how you think about the trade-offs you make every day. The 5am alarm for early productivity is costing you the creativity and emotional regulation of your final sleep cycle. These are real costs. Understanding them is what makes you willing to protect the sleep you have.

*　*　*

The Method: CALCULATING YOUR SLEEP WINDOW Your sleep window is the specific block of time — beginning at a consistent bed time and ending at a consistent wake time — during which your brain will cycle through its full sleep architecture.

To calculate yours, work backward from your wake time. If your wake time is 6:30am and you need eight hours, your sleep onset time should be 10:30pm. Add 15 to 20 minutes for the time it takes to fall asleep, and your bedtime is approximately 10:10pm.

The mathematical reality of sleep staging means that extending your night by 90 minutes does not just give you 90 more minutes of light sleep. It gives you an additional near-complete sleep cycle — including a full REM period — that produces disproportionate improvements in mood, memory, and cognitive function the following day.

*　*　*

The Exercise Tonight, calculate your sleep window.

Write down: your consistent wake time, the number of hours you need (most adults: seven to nine), your target sleep onset time (wake time minus sleep need), and your bedtime (sleep onset time minus 20 minutes). Write these four numbers somewhere visible. Not as a rigid rule but as a target — a destination for tonight and every night for the next two weeks.

*　*　*

Chapter Summary

Sleep cycles through four distinct stages — light sleep, slow-wave, and REM — in repeating cycles of approximately 90 minutes. Each stage performs different restorative functions.

Slow-wave sleep (physical repair, brain waste clearance) is concentrated in the first half of the night. REM sleep (memory, emotion, creativity) is concentrated in the second half.

Cutting your night short disproportionately eliminates REM sleep. Extend your night by going to bed earlier, not waking later.

Six hours per night for two weeks produces cognitive impairment equivalent to 48 hours without sleep — invisible to the person experiencing it. Alcohol suppresses REM sleep. The relaxation at bedtime is real; the sleep architecture damage is equally real.

Chapter 3

Your Sleep Environment — The Signals Your Bedroom Sends

Your bedroom is currently sending signals. Not metaphorical ones. Biological ones — precise, measurable signals that your nervous system reads before you are even conscious of processing them, and that either prepare your brain for sleep or actively work against it. The temperature of the room. The quality and spectrum of the light. The presence of the phone on the nightstand. The sounds that are or are not present. Every one of these is a cue. Your brain is responding to all of them simultaneously.

And in most people's bedrooms, most of those signals are wrong.

* * *

The Problem The bedroom has become a multi-purpose room. It is where you work late when the deadline is close. Where you scroll before sleep and immediately after waking. Where you have difficult conversations because it is the only private space available. Where the television lives, and the charger, and the laptop, and the phone.

Over time — through classical conditioning that operates completely below conscious awareness — your brain has learned to associate the bedroom with wakefulness, activity, and stimulation. The bed, which should be the most powerful sleep trigger in your environment, has become associated with everything except sleep.

This is not a metaphor. It is a well-documented neurological process called stimulus control, and it is one of the most reliably reversible contributors to poor sleep in modern adults.

* * *

The Science Temperature is the most important environmental factor for sleep onset and sleep depth. Research by Eus van Someren at the Netherlands Institute for Neuroscience established that core body temperature must drop by approximately 1 to 1.5 degrees Celsius from its daily peak for sleep onset to occur. The body achieves this drop by dilating blood vessels in the hands and feet — radiating heat outward and cooling the core. The ideal bedroom temperature to support this process is 65 to 68 degrees Fahrenheit (18 to 20 degrees Celsius). Rooms that are warmer impair the body's ability to drop its core temperature, delaying sleep onset and reducing slow-wave sleep depth. Light is the second critical variable. The specialized cells in your retina that drive circadian rhythm — intrinsically photosensitive retinal ganglion cells — are maximally sensitive to short-wavelength blue light, which is precisely the spectrum emitted by LED screens and energy-efficient bulbs. Research by Charles Czeisler at Harvard Medical School found that two hours of tablet use before bed delayed melatonin onset by 90 minutes, delayed sleep onset by 45 minutes, and shifted the circadian clock forward — effects that persisted into the following day.

Sound matters differently than most people expect. The issue is not silence — research does not support that sleeping in total silence is better than sleeping with consistent background sound. The issue is acoustic unpredictability. Sudden sounds — a phone notification, a car alarm, a partner's alarm in another room — trigger brief arousal responses even during deep sleep, fragmenting sleep architecture without the sleeper being aware of waking. Consistent, low-level background noise (white noise, pink noise, or a fan) masks these acoustic spikes, producing measurably more consolidated sleep in environments where intermittent noise is unavoidable.

*   *   *

The Reframe Your bedroom is not just where you sleep. It is the primary sleep-triggering environment your brain has available. Every non-sleep activity that takes place there weakens that association — and every sleep-promoting modification strengthens it.

A brain that enters a bedroom consistently used only for sleep and intimacy begins initiating sleep-onset physiology — dropping body temperature, releasing melatonin, reducing cognitive arousal — before you are even in the bed. That is the goal. And it is achievable in two weeks of consistent practice.

* * *

The Concept: THE THREE ENVIRONMENTAL LEVERS Temperature. Set your thermostat to 65 to 68 degrees Fahrenheit before bed. If you cannot control your bedroom temperature directly, use lighter bedding, open a window, or use a fan for airflow. Keep hands and feet uncovered and slightly cool to accelerate core temperature drop. If your room is too cold, warm socks before bed help — warming the feet accelerates vasodilation and core temperature drop, paradoxically helping you fall asleep faster. Light. Two changes, both non-negotiable. First, dim the lights in your living space beginning 90 minutes before your target bedtime. Second, eliminate all light from the bedroom during sleep. Blackout curtains or a sleep mask — any residual light, including the LED standby light on electronics, measurably reduces melatonin levels and reduces sleep depth. The bedroom during sleep should be dark enough that you cannot see your hand in front of your face. The phone. This is not primarily a screen-time issue. It is a stimulus control issue. The phone on the nightstand is both a source of light and sound disruption and a powerful psychological association with wakefulness. Remove it from the bedroom entirely. Charge it in another room. Buy an alarm clock. This single change addresses multiple sleep disruptors simultaneously.

* * *

The Method: THE BEDROOM AUDIT Walk through your bedroom tonight with fresh eyes. Assess it against three standards.

Is it cool enough? If your bedroom is above 68 degrees Fahrenheit during sleep hours, you are sleeping in a space that is physiologically impeding your body's temperature-drop mechanism.

Is it dark enough? In complete darkness, you should not be able to see your hand in front of your face. If you can see any light source — any — your melatonin production is being suppressed.

Is the phone in the room? If yes, this is the most important change you can make. Move it out tonight.

* * *

The Exercise Make one physical change to your bedroom tonight. Not all three — one. If your room is too warm: open a window, adjust the thermostat, or replace heavy bedding with lighter alternatives.

If your room is too bright: buy a sleep mask or hang blackout fabric over any windows that allow light in.

If your phone is in the bedroom: move it to the hallway, the kitchen, or another room. You can hear an alarm through a closed door.

One change. Tonight.

* * *

Chapter Summary

Your bedroom sends biological signals your brain reads before you are consciously aware of processing them. Most modern bedrooms send the wrong signals — associating the bed with wakefulness.

The bedroom should be 65 to 68 degrees Fahrenheit. Your body needs to drop its core temperature by 1 to 1.5 degrees Celsius for sleep onset to occur. Blue-spectrum light from screens suppresses melatonin and delays sleep onset by 45 minutes. The bedroom during sleep must be completely dark. Remove the phone from the bedroom. This single action addresses light disruption, acoustic disruption, and the conditioned association between the bed and wakefulness.

Consistent background noise (fan, white noise) produces more consolidated sleep in environments with unpredictable acoustic disruptions.

Chapter 4

The Wind-Down Window — 90 Minutes That Change Everything

There is a version of you that falls asleep within ten minutes of getting into bed. Not because you are exhausted. Because your body has been preparing for sleep for the past 90 minutes. Your cortisol has been declining steadily since you began dimming the lights and putting down the phone. Your core body temperature has started its descent. Your melatonin is rising. Every signal your brain has received in the past hour and a half has said: the day is ending, the body is safe, sleep is coming.

That version of you is not rare. It is what sleep looks like when the conditions are right. The 90 minutes before bed are those conditions.

* * *

The Problem Most people have no wind-down routine. They work until they are tired — or they scroll until they are tired, which is different, because screen stimulation creates a shallow alertness that mimics tiredness without the adenosine pressure that produces genuine sleepiness — and then they get into bed and expect the transition from full activation to sleep to happen instantly. It cannot. The nervous system does not switch states instantaneously. Cortisol does not drop on command. The sympathetic nervous system — governing fight-or- flight — takes time to yield to the parasympathetic system that governs rest. That transition requires an intermediate state: a period of low stimulation, declining light, and physical and cognitive deceleration.

The absence of that intermediate state is one of the most common and most fixable causes of sleep-onset difficulty in adults.

* * *

The Science Research on pre-sleep arousal — the physiological and cognitive activation state that precedes sleep — identifies it as one of the strongest predictors of sleep onset difficulty in otherwise healthy adults. A review by Markus Jansson-Fröjmark at Karolinska Institute found that pre-sleep arousal was the most consistent predictor of sleep onset difficulty across age groups, health conditions, and sleep environments.

The mechanism is clear. Cortisol and melatonin are mutually antagonistic — high cortisol suppresses melatonin release. Any activity in the 60 to 90 minutes before bed that maintains or elevates cortisol delays or blunts the melatonin rise that signals the body to initiate sleep physiology. Research by Kenneth Wright at the University of Colorado found that even moderate psychological stress in the evening — not clinical anxiety, just the normal activation of email, news, and unfinished tasks — elevates cortisol sufficiently to delay sleep onset by 20 to 40 minutes and reduce slow-wave sleep depth in the first sleep cycle.

Michael Scullin's lab at Baylor University showed that spending five minutes writing a detailed to-do list for the next day — a forward-looking list rather than a reflection on the day — reduced sleep onset latency by nine minutes on average. The act of writing externalizes the mental load, signaling to the brain that the information is captured and does not need to be actively held.

* * *

The Reframe The 90 minutes before bed are not wasted time. They are an investment in the quality of the next eight hours — the preparation that determines whether sleep onset takes ten minutes or forty-five. Whether your first sleep cycle is deep and restorative or shallow and fragmented. Whether you wake at 3am with a mind that immediately begins running.

The framing shift is this: the wind-down window is not the absence of your evening. It is the most important part of it. The work you do in those 90 minutes — not cognitively demanding work, but the specific restorative work of deceleration — is what makes everything that follows possible.

The Concept: THE 90-MINUTE PROTOCOL The most effective pre-sleep protocol has three distinct phases. The first phase: reduce cognitive arousal (60 minutes before sleep onset). Stop all work. Close the laptop. If unfinished tasks are creating cognitive intrusion, do a brief "brain dump": write down everything occupying your mind, followed by tomorrow's to-do list. Five minutes of writing to externalize mental load.

The second phase: reduce physiological arousal (45 minutes before sleep onset). Lower the lights significantly — transition to warm-spectrum lighting. If possible, have a warm bath or shower: immersion in warm water raises skin temperature, and when you exit the bath, the rapid core temperature drop is one of the most reliably effective sleep-onset triggers in the research.

The third phase: engage the parasympathetic system (30 minutes before sleep onset). Light reading of physical books. Gentle stretching. Breathing exercises. Any low-stimulation activity that is not cognitively demanding and does not involve screens.

* * *

The Method: YOUR WIND-DOWN TRIGGER A wind-down protocol only works if it starts consistently. The challenge is not the protocol — the protocol is simple — it is the trigger. Choose a specific, recurring time that signals the beginning of your 90-minute window. Not "when I feel tired." A specific time, anchored to your target sleep onset time. If your target sleep onset is 10:30pm, your wind-down trigger is 9:00pm.

At 9:00pm — every night — you stop work, lower the lights, and begin the transition. The consistency of the trigger is what builds the habit. And the habit is what eventually makes the wind-down feel effortless.

* * *

The Exercise Tonight, try one element of the 90-minute protocol.

Specifically: one hour before your target sleep time, write a five-minute to-do list for tomorrow. Detailed, specific, and forward-looking. Everything you need to do, in the order you plan to do it.

Then close the notebook, put it somewhere you will see it in the morning, and do something non-cognitively demanding until bed.

Tomorrow night, add the light-dimming. The night after, add the screen-off rule. Build the protocol one element at a time.

* * *

Chapter Summary

The nervous system does not switch from full activation to sleep instantaneously. The 90 minutes before bed are the transition period during which cortisol must decline and melatonin must rise — and most people skip this transition entirely.

Pre-sleep cognitive and physiological arousal is the most consistent predictor of sleep-onset difficulty in otherwise healthy adults. The 90-minute wind-down protocol has three phases: reduce cognitive arousal, reduce physiological arousal, engage the parasympathetic system. Writing a forward-looking to-do list five minutes before bed reduces sleep onset latency by approximately nine minutes by externalizing mental load. Choose a specific, consistent trigger time — not "when I feel tired." Consistency builds the habit.

Chapter 5

The Morning Anchor — Why Your Night Starts at Dawn

The most powerful thing you can do for tonight's sleep has nothing to do with tonight. It happens tomorrow morning. Within thirty minutes of waking. Before coffee. Before your phone. Before anything else competing for the first moments of your day.

You go outside. Or you stand at a bright window. And you let natural light reach your eyes for ten to thirty minutes.

That is it. That is the intervention. And it is so biologically powerful that sleep researchers consistently identify it as the single most effective circadian-resetting intervention available without medical treatment.

* * *

The Problem Most modern adults spend the first hours of their day in artificial light — the dim, warm-spectrum light of a kitchen, or the bright blue light of a phone screen. Neither provides the stimulus that the circadian system needs to anchor itself to the day.

The circadian clock requires a light signal of approximately 10,000 lux to reset itself each morning. A sunny outdoor environment provides 50,000 to 100,000 lux. A brightly lit indoor room provides 200 to 500 lux. Without the morning light anchor, the circadian clock drifts — typically delaying by 15 to 30 minutes per day. After two weeks of insufficient morning light exposure, the mismatch between your biological clock and your desired sleep schedule can be significant enough to explain most of the sleep-onset difficulty you have been attributing to other causes.

* * *

The Science The mechanism operates through the suprachiasmatic nucleus (SCN) — the master circadian clock — which receives direct light input from specialized retinal cells and uses it to synchronize all the body's peripheral clocks to a consistent 24-hour rhythm.

When the SCN receives a robust morning light signal, it initiates a cascade: cortisol is released in a sharp morning pulse (the cortisol awakening response, or CAR), which drives alertness for the first hours of the day. Approximately 12 to 14 hours later — precisely, based on the timing of the morning light signal — the SCN initiates melatonin release, signaling the onset of biological night.

Research by Satchin Panda at the Salk Institute found that the timing of the morning light signal predicts the timing of the melatonin onset that evening with remarkable consistency. A morning light signal received at 7am reliably produces melatonin onset around 9pm, creating the biological conditions for easy sleep onset at 10 to 11pm. A morning spent indoors without adequate light exposure produces a blunted, delayed melatonin onset — and a night of lying in bed awake, wondering why sleep will not come. Till Roenneberg's work at Ludwig Maximilian University of Munich has found that social jetlag — circadian misalignment produced by irregular wake times — is associated with significantly higher rates of sleep difficulties, metabolic disruption, and mood disturbance. The weekend sleep-in that feels like recovery is, in circadian terms, shifting your clock forward by hours and requiring days of adjustment.

* * *

The Reframe Most people approach sleep as an evening problem — something to be managed at bedtime with supplements, routines, and the right mattress. The research says sleep is a 24-hour system with a morning anchor. You cannot reliably produce easy 10pm sleep onset if you are spending your mornings in dim indoor light. The morning anchor is the foundation that the evening routines rest on. Without it, the rest of the advice in this book is less effective than it should be.

* * *

The Concept: THE THREE MORNING RULES Get outdoor light within 30 minutes of waking. Before coffee. Before your phone. Walk to the end of your street and back. Stand on the porch. Have breakfast near a window. The light signal must reach your eyes — it does not require direct sunlight or sunny weather. Even overcast outdoor light delivers 1,000 to 10,000 lux — ten to fifty times more than indoor artificial light. Don't take caffeine for at least 90 minutes after waking. In the first 90 minutes after waking, your cortisol awakening response is at its daily peak. Caffeine during this period is redundant — your natural alerting hormones are already at maximum. Delaying caffeine by 90 minutes preserves more adenosine build-up that will contribute to genuine sleep pressure that evening, and produces a stronger alerting effect from the same caffeine dose. Keep your wake time consistent. Already established in Chapter 1, this is worth re-emphasizing here: variation greater than one hour — including weekends — produces social jetlag. The weekend sleep-in is not recovery. It is circadian disruption that requires days of adjustment.

*   *   *

The Method: THE MORNING LIGHT HABIT STACK Attach the morning light behavior to something you already do every morning. Option 1: Take your morning coffee outside for ten to fifteen minutes. Option 2: Walk to the coffee shop instead of making coffee at home. Option 3: Have breakfast directly in front of your largest window with the blinds fully open.

Whatever form it takes, the behavior needs to happen within 30 minutes of waking and before the first extended screen interaction of the day.

*   *   *

The Exercise Tomorrow morning, set an additional alarm 15 minutes after your wake alarm. When the second alarm goes off, you should be outside — or standing at a window with the blinds fully open. Stay there for ten minutes. If it is raining or cold, dress appropriately. The light still works through cloud cover. Do this for seven consecutive mornings. On day seven, notice whether your evening sleepiness — the natural pull toward sleep in the hour before your target bedtime — feels stronger than it did on day one. It will.

* * *

Chapter Summary

Your circadian rhythm requires a morning light signal of approximately 10,000 lux to anchor itself accurately. Outdoor light, even overcast, delivers this. Indoor light does not.

The timing of your morning light signal determines the timing of your evening melatonin onset. Get outdoor light at 7am and your biology will be ready for sleep at 10pm.

Delay caffeine by 90 minutes after waking to preserve the natural cortisol awakening response and build genuine adenosine pressure for the evening. Consistent wake time prevents social jetlag — the circadian equivalent of crossing time zones every weekend.

Stack the morning light behavior onto an existing habit to make it automatic.

Chapter 6

Food, Drink, and Sleep — What Science Actually Says

There is more misinformation about sleep and nutrition than about almost any other area of sleep science. Melatonin is widely sold as a sleep aid — and it is largely ineffective for the sleep problems most people have. Chamomile tea is soothing — but there is no robust evidence that it meaningfully improves sleep architecture in healthy adults. Meanwhile, the substances that most consistently and significantly disrupt sleep are the ones most adults consume daily, in quantities they have no idea are problematic, at times they have no idea are harmful.

Here is what the research actually says.

* * *

The Problem Most adults are making at least one dietary or beverage choice every day that measurably disrupts their sleep — and they have no idea. Everyone knows that coffee before bed is a bad idea. Most people do not know that a coffee at 2pm is still half-active at 9pm and is reducing their slow-wave sleep depth even when they fall asleep without difficulty. Almost nobody knows that alcohol — widely used as a sleep aid — profoundly disrupts the sleep architecture it appears to facilitate.

This chapter will make the science specific. Specific enough to change what you eat and drink today.

* * *

The Science Caffeine is the most important dietary factor in sleep quality for the vast majority of adults. Its half-life in the average adult is five to seven hours, but there is significant individual variation: fast metabolizers process caffeine in three to four hours, while slow metabolizers may carry it for nine to twelve hours after consumption.

If you regularly sleep poorly despite otherwise good sleep habits and you consume caffeine after noon, your metabolism may be slow. Try stopping at noon for one week and observe the difference.

Alcohol is the most damaging dietary substance for sleep quality and the one most consistently misunderstood. Alcohol is a sedative — it shortens sleep onset latency and produces a state of reduced arousal that is easily misidentified as good sleep. What it actually produces is sedation, not sleep, and the two are not neurologically equivalent.

Matthew Walker's summary of the alcohol-sleep research is precise: alcohol suppresses REM sleep in the first half of the night. As the alcohol metabolizes during the second half, the brain rebounds from REM suppression — producing a second half of broken, vivid, disturbing sleep. Alcohol at bedtime is not a sleep aid. It is a sleep disruptor that accelerates sleep onset while damaging every aspect of sleep quality that follows.

Melatonin deserves specific attention because it is so widely used and so frequently misapplied. Melatonin is not a sleep-inducing drug — it is a circadian signal. It tells your brain that darkness has arrived, nudging the circadian clock toward sleep. It does not force sleep, and it does not enhance sleep architecture.

When melatonin is appropriate, the typical supplement dose (3 to 10mg) is drastically higher than what the research supports. Randomised controlled trials have consistently found that doses of 0.1 to 0.3mg produce equivalent or superior circadian effects compared to high doses.

Research on evening eating and sleep found that large meals within two hours of bedtime elevate core body temperature, increase metabolic rate, and activate digestion — all of which impede the temperature drop required for sleep onset. Magnesium glycinate stands out as the most evidence-supported supplement for sleep quality in adults who may be deficient — a significant proportion of the population, given that magnesium is depleted by stress, coffee, and processed food consumption. The effective dose is 300 to 400mg of magnesium glycinate — not magnesium oxide, which is poorly absorbed — taken 30 minutes before bed.

The Reframe The dietary conversation about sleep has been dominated by what to add — which supplements to take, which herbal teas to drink. The research consistently shows that the more important question is what to remove and when. Removing afternoon caffeine restores sleep pressure more effectively than any supplement. Removing alcohol removes one of the most reliably destructive forces on sleep architecture in a standard Western diet. These are subtractions — and subtractions are almost always easier to implement than additions.

* * *

The Concept: THE DIETARY SLEEP WINDOW Think of the dietary decisions that affect sleep as falling within a specific window: the eight hours before your target sleep onset time. In the first four hours of that window (roughly mid-afternoon), the primary decision is caffeine timing. After your individual caffeine cutoff time — established by your metabolism, not an arbitrary rule — switch to non- caffeinated alternatives.

In the middle two hours of that window (early evening), the primary decision is meal size and composition. Eat a moderate dinner that completes at least two hours before your target sleep time.

In the final two hours, avoid alcohol and large meals. Alcohol should be complete at least three hours before sleep if consumed.

* * *

The Method: YOUR CAFFEINE EXPERIMENT For the next seven days, move your caffeine cutoff time two hours earlier than your current cutoff.

If you currently have your last coffee at 4pm, move it to 2pm. If you currently stop at 2pm, move it to noon.

Note any change in time to fall asleep, number of awakenings, and how rested you feel in the morning. If you notice significant improvement, your current cutoff was too late for your metabolism. Maintain the earlier cutoff permanently.

The Exercise Tonight, before you eat or drink anything in the evening, answer three questions: What time is it right now, and when is my target sleep onset? Is there caffeine in what I'm about to consume?

Will I have finished this meal or drink at least two hours before sleep? These three questions are a filter — a moment of awareness between impulse and action. That awareness, applied consistently, produces better dietary sleep decisions without requiring willpower.

* * *

Chapter Summary

Caffeine has a five-to-seven-hour half-life. Your caffeine cutoff should be established by your individual metabolism — try stopping two hours earlier for one week to identify the right time for you.

Alcohol is not a sleep aid. It suppresses REM sleep, fragments sleep in the second half of the night, and produces measurably worse sleep quality overall. Complete alcohol consumption at least three hours before sleep. Standard melatonin doses (3 to 10mg) are far too high. When melatonin is appropriate, 0.1 to 0.3mg produces equivalent or superior effects. Avoid large, high-fat meals within two hours of your target sleep time. Digestion competes with the body temperature drop required for sleep onset. Magnesium glycinate (300 to 400mg before bed) is the most evidence-supported dietary supplement for sleep quality in deficient adults.

Chapter 7

When Your Mind Won't Stop — Breaking the Anxiety Loop

Here is the cruelest thing about sleep anxiety. The anxiety is caused by not sleeping. And the anxiety makes it harder to sleep. Which creates more anxiety. Which makes sleep harder still. You know this loop. You've been in it — at 1am, at 2am, at 3am, calculating how many hours you will get if you fall asleep right now, which makes it harder to fall asleep, which changes the calculation. You've tried to stop thinking about it and found that trying to stop thinking about something is the most reliable way to ensure you keep thinking about it.

The loop is real. The anxiety is real. And there is a way out of it — not through willpower, not through positive thinking, but through understanding the specific mechanisms that create and sustain the loop and applying the specific techniques that interrupt them.

* * *

The Problem Sleep anxiety is a learned response. It begins with a period of poor sleep — triggered by stress, illness, a time zone change, a new baby, or any ordinary life disruption — and it self-perpetuates through a specific cognitive and physiological mechanism.

Poor sleep creates fatigue. Fatigue creates concern about tonight's sleep. That concern creates arousal — a mild but measurable activation of the stress response — that elevates cortisol in the evening. The elevated cortisol makes tonight's sleep worse. Which creates more concern. Which creates more evening arousal.

Meanwhile, the bedroom has become associated with lying awake and feeling anxious — through classical conditioning, below conscious awareness — which means that the act of entering the bedroom, getting into bed, and turning off the light now triggers the same cortisol elevation that the anxious thoughts create.

Breaking this loop requires two things: interrupting the cognitive cycle of worry and rumination, and breaking the conditioned association between the bed and wakefulness.

* * *

The Science The cognitive shuffle, developed by cognitive scientist Luc P. Beaudoin at Simon Fraser University, works by deliberately generating a sequence of random, unconnected images in a way that mimics the disorganised, associative thinking the brain produces just before sleep onset. The random imagery prevents the linear, narrative thinking that constitutes worry and problem-solving, and the brain, mistaking the random imagery for the pre-sleep state, begins initiating sleep physiology. In Beaudoin's published research, participants using the technique fell asleep measurably faster than those using standard relaxation techniques, with most reporting sleep onset within 20 minutes of beginning the exercise. Constructive worry, developed by researchers at Concordia University, channels the tendency to ruminate into a brief, structured, pre-bedtime exercise. Rather than trying to suppress worrying thoughts — which increases their frequency through what Daniel Wegner called the "ironic process theory" — constructive worry has you write down specific worries and one concrete action for each. Research found that this exercise significantly reduced the frequency and duration of intrusive worry thoughts during the sleep period. Stimulus control therapy, developed by sleep researcher Richard Bootzin, is the single most effective non-pharmaceutical intervention for chronic sleep- onset difficulties. The principle is simple: the bed should be used only for sleep and intimacy. If you are in bed and not asleep within 20 minutes, get up. Go to another room. Sit in dim light and do something non-stimulating until you feel sleepy. Then return to bed.

This instruction feels counterintuitive and punitive to most people who encounter it. The research is unambiguous: stimulus control therapy works by re-establishing the conditioned association between the bed and sleep that anxiety had eroded. Its effects persist long after the intervention ends.

The Reframe The anxious thoughts that circle at 3am are not insights. They are not useful preparation. They are the output of a brain operating in threat mode — a mode designed for short-term survival, not problem-solving or rest. The brain under sleep deprivation and anxiety is not a reliable narrator. The problems that feel catastrophic at 2am feel manageable at 8am. This is not because the problems have changed. It is because the sleep-deprived, cortisol-flooded brain exaggerates threat and loses the capacity for proportionate assessment.

The thoughts that prevent sleep are not telling you something important that needs attending right now. They are the symptom of a brain that needs sleep. And the fastest way to get sleep is to stop engaging with them — not to suppress them, which makes them louder, but to replace them with something they cannot compete with.

* * *

The Concept: BREAKING THE LOOP IN REAL TIME The cognitive shuffle works by preventing the linear thinking that sustains the anxiety loop. When you get into bed and your mind begins to run, begin generating random, unconnected mental images. Make them specific and concrete: a green umbrella leaning against a yellow wall. A crow on a telephone wire. A child's blue mitten on a snowy step. A wooden spoon in a glass jar. The images should be random — unconnected to each other and to anything in your actual life. They should be visual — pictures, not words. And they should be gentle, ordinary, and slightly surreal.

When a worry thought intrudes — and it will — don't fight it. Simply return to the image sequence. A cracked ceramic bowl. A yellow taxi. A field of sunflowers.

Most people who try this experience some version of this: they begin the exercise, get distracted by a worry, return to the images, and then — without noticing the transition — find themselves waking briefly and realizing they were asleep. The technique cannot maintain worry-thinking while simultaneously generating random associative imagery. Choose the imagery. Let the thinking stop on its own.

The Method: Two protocols. Do both, in this order.

Protocol one: the constructive worry session Run this in the hour before bed — not in bed, before bed. Sitting at a table or desk, with a pen and paper.

Step one: set a timer for ten minutes.

Step two: write down every concern currently circulating in your mind. Not an edited or organized version — every unresolved thought that might visit you tonight. The work situation. The conversation that did not go well. The appointment you have not made. The thing you said and are still turning over. Write without filtering until either the timer ends or the page is empty. Step three: for each item, write one specific, concrete next action. Not a solution. One next action. "Call the insurance company Thursday morning." "Draft the email and save it as a draft." "Look up the appointment number." The action does not need to resolve the concern. It needs to be specific enough that your brain can release the item from active monitoring, knowing it has been handed off to a future version of you who has a plan. Step four: close the notebook. Place it somewhere visible. This is deliberate — it signals that the concerns exist outside your head, recorded and tended to, and do not require your memory to preserve them overnight. Step five: do not open the notebook again until the following morning. The whole protocol takes ten to fifteen minutes. Research consistently shows that specificity matters — vague intentions ("I should deal with that") do not close cognitive loops. Concrete next actions do.

Protocol two: the 20-minute bed rule This protocol rebuilds the conditioned association between bed and sleep that anxiety has eroded. It requires consistency over time — one to two weeks of application before the full effect establishes. It is not comfortable at first. It is the most evidence-supported non-pharmaceutical intervention available for sleep-onset difficulties.

The rule: if you are in bed, awake, and not feeling the physical pull toward sleep after twenty minutes — get up.

Not "a while." Twenty minutes. Use a non-phone clock visible from the bed. When you get up, leave the bedroom entirely. Go to a dim room. Sit quietly — reading a physical book, doing gentle stretching, listening to something calm with your eyes closed. No screens. No phone. No stimulating content of any kind. Keep the lighting dim.

The activity doesn't need to be productive. Its only function is to occupy you without arousing you while you wait for genuine sleepiness to return. When you notice the physical signs of sleepiness — heavy eyelids, slowing thoughts, the involuntary pull toward lying down — return to bed. Not before. Repeat as many times as necessary. Some nights, in the first week, this means getting up two or three times. That is correct. The disruption is temporary. The conditioning it produces is lasting. Within ten to fourteen nights of consistent application, most people find that lying down in bed reliably triggers the transition toward sleep rather than the alert scanning of the sleepless.

* * *

The Exercise Tonight, before you get into bed, spend ten minutes on constructive worry. Take a pen and paper — not your phone — and write down every thought that might intrude on your sleep tonight. The work deadline. The unresolved conversation. The financial concern. For each one, write down one specific action — not a solution, just the next concrete step.

Close the notebook. Put it somewhere you will see it tomorrow. Then get into bed. If the thoughts return, begin the cognitive shuffle. Random images. An orange kite tangled in a maple tree. A white cat on a blue chair. A glass of water on a stone windowsill.

Let the thinking go. Let sleep find you.

* * *

Chapter Summary

Sleep anxiety is a learned, self-perpetuating loop: poor sleep creates anxiety about sleep, which elevates evening cortisol, which disrupts sleep. Breaking the loop requires interrupting the cognitive cycle and the conditioned association between bed and wakefulness.

Constructive worry — ten minutes before bed, writing worries with one concrete next action for each — significantly reduces intrusive night-time thinking. The cognitive shuffle — generating random, unconnected visual images — prevents the linear thinking that sustains anxiety and mimics the pre-sleep hypnagogic state.

The 20-minute rule (get up if not asleep after 20 minutes) is the single most effective non-pharmaceutical intervention for sleep-onset anxiety. Trying to suppress worrying thoughts increases their frequency. Replace them with random imagery or externalize them onto paper before bed.

Conclusion

Two Weeks from Now Two weeks is not a long time. It is fourteen nights.

In two weeks of consistently implemented changes — the consistent wake time, the morning light exposure, the caffeine cutoff, the wind-down window, the darkened room, the phone outside the bedroom, the pre-sleep worry journal — something measurable will have shifted. Not because these are powerful interventions in isolation, though several of them are. Because they are a system — each one addressing a specific disruption in the two biological systems that govern sleep, each one reinforcing the others.

The circadian rhythm, re-anchored by consistent wake times and morning light, will begin producing melatonin at a more consistent and appropriate hour. The sleep pressure system, no longer blunted by afternoon caffeine, will arrive at bedtime with the accumulated weight it is supposed to carry. The sleep environment, cleared of light disruption and the wakefulness associations of the phone, will begin signaling sleep to a brain that is ready to receive it. The wind-down window will give the nervous system the time it needs to complete the cortisol-to-melatonin transition. None of this requires perfection. Consistency, not perfection, is what the biological system responds to.

* * *

Here is what two weeks of consistent practice typically produces. Sleep onset latency decreases. The forty-five minutes of lying awake becomes twenty, then ten, then the unremarkable five to ten minutes that most people with healthy sleep patterns experience as the ordinary boundary between wakefulness and sleep.

Night awakenings become less frequent. The 3am waking that turns into an hour of anxious thought becomes a brief surfacing — a few minutes, a quiet awareness of the room, and then sleep again.

Morning grogginess decreases. Not because the alarm no longer exists, but because you are waking during a lighter sleep stage — aligned with your circadian rhythm — rather than being torn from deep sleep by a timer that knows nothing about your architecture.

And the subjective experience of the day changes. The cognitive fog that felt permanent lifts. The emotional reactivity that seemed like your personality becomes less pronounced. The creativity that you assumed had peaked returns. These are documented effects of moving from chronic partial sleep deprivation to adequate, well-structured sleep.

* * *

There is one more thing to understand before you close this book. Sleep is not a performance metric. The obsessive pursuit of perfect sleep — tracking every minute with a wearable device, fretting over each percentage point of sleep efficiency — produces its own form of arousal that undermines the very thing it is trying to improve. There is a name for this condition: orthosomnia. And it is more common than most people know.

The goal is not perfect sleep. The goal is good enough sleep — consistently. Not every night will be a good night. A bad night does not mean the system is broken. It means the system is human.

What you now have is a precise understanding of what drives that system and what disrupts it. You can use that understanding without becoming enslaved to it. You can implement these changes without demanding immediate perfection. You can have the occasional late night, the occasional glass of wine, the occasional morning where the outdoor light happens twenty minutes later than planned — and know that none of these is catastrophic. The system is resilient and the habits you are building are cumulative.

Go to bed. Turn off the phone. Trust the biology.

Two weeks from now, you will sleep like you mean it.

About the Author

Elias Grant writes practical, research-backed books on the specific micro-skills that most improve daily life. He focuses on the gap between knowing what would help and actually being able to do it — translating the best available research in psychology, neuroscience, and behavioral science into plain English and tools that work in ordinary, busy, imperfect lives. The Content 7 series is published by Asher Rohi Publishing.

Also by Asher Rohi Publishing

- Book 1 — Ask Better Questions:
  The One Skill That Improves Every Relationship and Meeting

- Book 2 — Sleep Like You Mean It:
  A No-Nonsense Guide to Better

- Rest Book 3 — Say No Without Guilt:
  How to Set Limits and Still Be

- Liked Book 4 — The 20-Minute Morning:
  A Simple System for Calm, Focused Days

- Book 5 — Read More, Remember More:
  How to Actually Finish Books and Use What You Learn

- Book 6 — Walk More, Live Better:
  How 30 Minutes a Day Changes Everything

- Book 7 — Digital Detox in 7 Days:
  Reclaim Your Focus Without Quitting the Internet

References

INTRODUCTION AND CHAPTER ONE

Walker, M. (2017). Why We Sleep: Unlocking the Power of Sleep and Dreams. Scribner.

Borbely, A. A. (1982). A two process model of sleep regulation. Human Neurobiology, 1(3), 195-204.

CHAPTER TWO

van der Helm, E., et al. (2011). REM sleep depotentiates amygdala activity to previous emotional experiences. Current Biology, 21(23), 2029-2032.

van Dongen, H. P., et al. (2003). The cumulative cost of additional wakefulness. Sleep, 26(2), 117-126.

CHAPTER THREE

van Someren, E. J. W. (2000). More than a marker: Interaction between the circadian regulation of temperature and sleep. Chronobiology International, 17(3), 313-354.

Chang, A. M., et al. (2015). Evening use of light-emitting eReaders negatively affects sleep. PNAS, 112(4), 1232-1237.

CHAPTER FOUR

Jansson-Frojmark, M., & Norell-Clarke, A. (2019). The cognitive model of insomnia. Sleep Medicine Reviews, 46, 75-91.

Scullin, M. K., et al. (2018). The effects of bedtime writing on difficulty falling asleep. Experimental Psychology: General, 147(1), 139-146.

CHAPTER FIVE

Panda, S. (2018). The Circadian Code. Rodale Books.

Roenneberg, T., et al. (2012). Social jetlag and obesity. Current Biology, 22(10), 939-943.

CHAPTER SIX

Walker, M. (2017). Op. cit.

Ferracioli-Oda, E., et al. (2013). Meta-analysis: Melatonin for the treatment of primary sleep disorders. PLOS ONE, 8(5), e63773.

CHAPTER SEVEN

Bootzin, R. R., & Perlis, M. L. (2011). Stimulus control therapy. In Behavioral Treatments for Sleep Disorders. Academic Press.

Harvey, A. G. (2002). A cognitive model of insomnia. Behavior Research and Therapy, 40(8), 869-893.

Wegner, D. M., et al. (1987). Paradoxical effects of thought suppression. Journal of Personality and Social Psychology, 53(1), 5-13.

Appendix: Companion Workbook

This appendix is your working space. It contains a worksheet for every chapter, a quick-reference card, and a fourteen-day quick-start plan to help you put the book into practice. You can write directly in your copy, or copy the prompts into a notebook — whichever feels easier. The most important rule is also the simplest: complete each worksheet the same day you read the chapter. The exercises are designed to be done immediately, not later. Most readers notice a real difference within two weeks of consistent application.

Chapter 1 Worksheet — Why You Can't Sleep

Key idea: Your sleep is governed by two systems: your circadian rhythm, driven by light, and your sleep pressure system, driven by adenosine. Most adult sleep problems fall into three categories: circadian misalignment, blunted sleep pressure from caffeine, and cortisol intrusion from stress or evening phone use. Your exercise: Set a consistent wake time for the next 14 days. The same time every day, including weekends. Set the alarm tonight before you sleep.

Reflection and application What time will my consistent wake time be?

____

My current last caffeine time:

____

My current screen-off time:

____

Which of the three disruptors is most likely affecting me? Circle one: circadian misalignment / blunted sleep pressure / cortisol intrusion / all three.

What specific habit is causing it?

____

Three-day sleep audit Before changing anything, track three days of your current sleep pattern.

Note last caffeine time, screen-off time, bed time, minutes to fall asleep, wake time, and how rested you feel out of 10.

Day 1:

____

Day 2:

____

Day 3:

____

Pattern I notice:

____

Chapter 2 Worksheet — What Actually Happens When You Sleep

Key idea: Sleep cycles through distinct stages in roughly ninety-minute cycles. Slow-wave sleep, which handles physical repair and brain waste clearance, clusters in the first half of the night. REM sleep, which handles memory, emotion, and creativity, clusters in the second half. Cutting your night short disproportionately removes REM. Six hours a night for two weeks equals 48 hours without sleep — invisible to you. Your exercise: Calculate your sleep window.

Write it down somewhere visible. Reflection and application My consistent wake time:

____

Hours of sleep I need (most adults need 7 to 9):

____

Target sleep onset time (wake time minus sleep need):

____

My bedtime (sleep onset minus 20 minutes for falling asleep):

____

Sleep architecture: what I am protecting Understanding what each stage does changes how seriously you protect your sleep window.

What I currently lose by going to bed late or waking early:

____

The cost of my early alarm is:

____

One trade-off I am willing to reconsider after this chapter:

____

Chapter 3 Worksheet — Your Sleep Environment

Key idea: Your bedroom sends biological signals your brain reads before you are conscious of processing them. Temperature (65 to 68°F), light (complete darkness), and phone placement are the three controllable levers. Stimulus control — using the bed only for sleep — is one of the most reliably reversible contributors to poor sleep. Your exercise: Make one physical change to your bedroom tonight. Not all three. One.

Reflection and application My bedroom temperature during sleep (estimate). Target: 65 to 68°F:

____

 Light level: can I see my hand in front of my face in the dark? Yes is a problem. No is correct. Is my phone in the bedroom? Yes or no:

____

The one change I will make tonight:

____

 Bedroom audit Walk through your bedroom now with these three questions.

Temperature {EMD} what will I change? Thermostat, lighter bedding, fan, window:

____

 Light — what will I change? Blackout curtain, sleep mask, cover LED standby lights:

____

Phone — where will I charge it instead of the bedroom?

———————————————————————

Other non-sleep associations I have built in this room (working, scrolling):

———————————————————————

One rule I will set for this room starting tonight:

———————————————————————

Chapter 4 Worksheet — The Wind-Down Window

Key idea: The 90 minutes before bed are not wasted time — they are the most important part of the evening. The nervous system cannot switch from full activation to sleep instantaneously. Cortisol must decline and melatonin must rise during this window. Most people skip this transition entirely. Your exercise: Tonight, one hour before your target sleep time, write a five-minute to-do list for tomorrow. Then close it and do something non-cognitively demanding.

Reflection and application My target sleep onset time:

____

My 90-minute wind-down trigger time:

____

What I currently do in the 90 minutes before bed (be honest):

____

The specific trigger I will use to begin wind-down each night:

____

What non-stimulating activity will I use during the wind-down? Reading, gentle stretching, bath, breathing — not screens.

____

The 90-minute protocol — my version Design your specific wind-down sequence. Keep it simple.

60 minutes before sleep onset, I will stop:

____

60 minutes before, I will also write tomorrow's to-do list (five minutes).
45 minutes before, I will dim lights and:

____

30 minutes before, I will:

____

My wind-down trigger time (set a recurring reminder):

____

Chapter 5 Worksheet — The Morning Anchor

Key idea: The timing of your morning light signal determines the timing of your evening melatonin onset. Morning light at 7am reliably produces melatonin onset around 9pm. Delay your morning light and you delay your ability to sleep that night. Delay caffeine by 90 minutes after waking to preserve the natural cortisol awakening response. Your exercise: Tomorrow morning, get outdoor light within 30 minutes of waking. Set a second alarm 15 minutes after your wake alarm as a reminder to go outside.

Reflection and application My wake time:

____

Light-exposure target: within 30 minutes of waking, by what time?

____

Where I currently spend the first 30 minutes after waking:

____

My habit stack: I will get morning light by attaching it to (take coffee outside, walk to coffee shop, breakfast by window):

____

Current first caffeine time:

____

New target (90 minutes after waking):

____

Seven-day morning light experiment Track your morning light practice for seven days. Note your evening sleepiness out of 10 on Day 7 versus Day 1. Use this format for each day: Got outside within 30 minutes (yes/no), first caffeine time, evening sleepiness (1 to 10).

Day 1:

____

Day 2:

____

Day 3:

____

Day 4:

____

Day 5:

____

Day 6:

____

Day 7:

____

Chapter 6 Worksheet — Food, Drink, and Sleep

Key idea: Caffeine has a five-to-seven-hour half-life. Your metabolism determines your cutoff. Alcohol is not a sleep aid: it suppresses REM and fragments the second half of the night. Standard melatonin doses (3 to 10mg) are too high — 0.1 to 0.3mg produces equivalent effects. Large meals within two hours of sleep impede temperature drop. Your exercise: Move your caffeine cutoff two hours earlier than your current cutoff for seven days. Note any change in sleep quality.

Reflection and application Current last caffeine time:

____

New experiment cutoff:

____

Do I use alcohol to help sleep? If yes, am I willing to test two alcohol-free weeks?

____

Do I eat within two hours of bedtime? Yes is worth changing. No is fine.

____

My dietary sleep window — what I will change first:

____

Seven-day caffeine experiment log Track your earlier caffeine cutoff and any change in sleep quality. For each day, note: last caffeine time, sleep onset in minutes, awakenings, and restedness out of 10.

Day 1:

———————————————————————————

Day 3:   54

———————————————————————————

Day 7:

———————————————————————————

Conclusion: was my previous cutoff too late? Yes, no, or no difference (may be a fast metabolizer).

———————————————————————————

Chapter 7 Worksheet — When Your Mind Won't Stop

Key idea: Sleep anxiety is a learned, self-perpetuating loop. Two evidence-based techniques interrupt it: constructive worry — write every concern plus one concrete next action before bed — and the 20-minute bed rule — if awake 20 minutes, get up, go to a dim room, return when truly sleepy. Both require 10 to 14 days of consistent application. Your exercise: Tonight, spend 10 minutes on constructive worry before bed. Write every concern circulating in your mind, then one specific next action for each.

Reflection and application Concerns circulating right now (write them all):

———————————————————————————————

———————————————————————————————

———————————————————————————————

 For each concern above, write one specific next action. Not a solution. One concrete step:

———————————————————————————————

———————————————————————————————

———————————————————————————————

Have I tried the 20-minute bed rule? If yes, what was the result?

____

Cognitive shuffle — practice Write five random, unconnected image sequences you could use tonight. They should be specific, visual, gentle, and unrelated to your life.

1.

____

2.

____

3.

____

4.

____

5.

____

Quick-Reference Sleep Card

The complete system at a glance.

Morning (first 30 minutes)

- Get outdoor light within 30 minutes of waking.
- Keep wake time consistent every day.
- Delay first caffeine 90 minutes after waking.

Afternoon

- Caffeine cutoff: six to eight hours before bedtime.
- Switch to water or herbal tea after cutoff.
- Light dinner, complete two hours before sleep.

Evening (90 minutes before bed)

- Dim lights, warm spectrum only.
- Screens off, phone out of bedroom.
- Write tomorrow's to-do list (five minutes).

In bed

- Cognitive shuffle if mind races.
- 20-minute rule: get up if not asleep.
- Room: 65 to 68°F, pitch dark.

Key numbers to remember

- 65 to 68°F: ideal bedroom temperature for sleep onset.
- 1 to 1.5°C: core body temperature drop needed for sleep onset.
- Five to seven hours: caffeine half-life (individual variation: three to twelve hours).
- 90 minutes: melatonin delay from two hours of tablet use before bed.

- 17 percent: reduction in slow-wave sleep from a 3pm coffee.
- 0.1 to 0.3mg: evidence-supported melatonin dose, not three to ten milligrams.
- 20 minutes: the bed rule — get up if not asleep after this.
- 10 to 14 days: time for stimulus control therapy to take full effect.
- Two weeks: time for consistent application to produce real results.

14-Day Quick-Start Plan

Your step-by-step implementation sequence.

Do not implement everything at once. Build each change into your routine before adding the next. This sequence prioritizes the changes with the fastest measurable results.

Days 1 to 2 — Set your consistent wake time Choose a wake time and set it as a recurring alarm for every day, including weekends. Do not change anything else yet. Just observe.

Days 3 to 4 — Morning light and caffeine delay Get outdoor light within 30 minutes of waking. Delay your first caffeine by 90 minutes. Track evening sleepiness out of 10.

Days 5 to 6 — Bedroom: phone out and temperature Move your phone to another room for charging. Set your bedroom temperature to 65 to 68°F or as close as possible.

Days 7 to 8 — Wind-down trigger Set a recurring alarm 90 minutes before your target sleep time. When it sounds, stop working and begin winding down. Start with just one element: writing tomorrow's to-do list.

Days 9 to 10 — Screen-off rule Add screens off at the wind-down trigger. Use physical books, gentle stretching, or quiet music in the wind-down window.

Days 11 to 12 — Caffeine cutoff adjustment Move your caffeine cutoff two hours earlier than your current cutoff. Track any change in sleep onset and depth.

Days 13 to 14 — Anxiety tools if needed If you are still experiencing sleep anxiety or a racing mind, add the constructive worry practice (10 minutes before bed) and the 20-minute bed rule.

Daily check-in tracker Check off each day as you complete your current focus change. For each day, note: wake time, morning light (yes/no), caffeine cutoff time, wind-down (yes/no), sleep onset in minutes, and how rested you feel out of 10.

Day 1:

____

Day 2:

____

Day 3:

____

Day 4:

____

Day 5:

____

Day 6:

____

Day 7:

Day 8:

Day 9:

Day 10:

Day 11:

Day 12:

Day 13:

Day 14:

Two weeks of consistent application. That is all this takes. The system is in your hands. Now go sleep like you mean it.

Disclaimer

This book is intended for general informational and educational purposes only. It is not a substitute for professional medical, psychological, or other professional advice. Always seek qualified professional guidance before making significant changes to your health, sleep, diet, exercise habits, or professional practices. The author and publisher disclaim any liability arising directly or indirectly from the use or application of any information contained in this book.

A note from the publisher Asher Rohi Publishing is an independent press producing short, research-backed books on the micro-skills that most improve daily life. Every book in the catalogue is designed to be read in a few sittings and applied immediately.

If this book was useful, the most valuable thing you can do for it is leave an honest review at Amazon or the bookseller of your choice. Reviews are how independent books find new readers — even one or two sentences make a real difference.

To explore the rest of the series, sign up for new releases, or contact the publisher, visit asherrohipublishing.com.

Published by Asher Rohi Publishing asherrohipublishing.com First Edition, 2026 A catalogue record for this book is available from the National Library of Australia.

Published by Asher Rohi Publishing

asherrohipublishing.com

First Edition, 2026